Silly Sammy and Dandy Davy Learn about Their Teeth

Written by: Az-u-c-it

PUBLISH AMERICA

PublishAmerica
Baltimore

First printing

ISBN: 9781462638666
PUBLISHED BY PUBLISHAMERICA, LLLP
www.publishamerica.com
Baltimore

Printed in the United States of America

Mouthwash
and
toothpaste
toothbrushes and floss,

**If
Silly Sammy & Dandy Davey
don't have
clean teeth
their teeth will be their loss.**

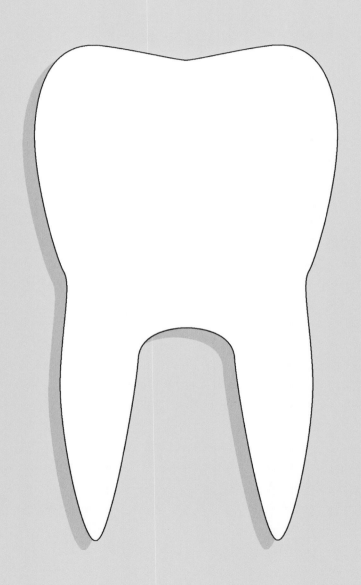

If
they
floss
daily
and brush three times a day,

**Their
teeth
will be
beautiful
and they will not have decay!**

Fruits
such
as
apples
and veggies like peas,

are
good
for
their
teeth...
...so Brush, if you please!

Sammy and Davey
felt
like
a big
girl and boy
for making their teeth so clean.

Sammy & Davey
smiled
their
biggest
smile
so everyone would've seen.

The
sparkle
and
shine
upon
their teeth
glowing so pearly white,

They'd
flossed
&
brushed
&
didn't
know....
They were a beautiful sight!!!

Would you like to see your manuscript become a book?

If you are interested in becoming a PublishAmerica author, please submit your manuscript for possible publication to us at:

acquisitions@publishamerica.com

You may also mail in your manuscript to:

**PublishAmerica
PO Box 151
Frederick, MD 21705**

www.publishamerica.com

CPSIA information can be obtained
at www.ICGtesting.com
Printed in the USA
429761LV00004B/12